DEALING WITH IMPOSSIBLE CLIENTS

What to Do When Clients Are Jerks, Deadbeats, Delusional, or Just Plain Crazy

by

Gini Graham Scott, Ph.D.

DEALING WITH IMPOSSIBLE CLIENTS

TABLE OF CONTENTS

OVERVIEW

Inevitably, small business owners, managers, professionals, and consultants encounter the extremely difficult client who comes in many shapes and sizes – ranging from "know-it-alls but don't know they don't know" to master manipulators, deadbeats, and con-artists. Such clients can sap your time, cost you money, alienate other clients, damage your reputation, and drive you nuts.

What do you do? Try to placate the client and bend over backwards to fill a request? Tell the client where to go, though diplomatically? Have a heart to heart? Discuss the problem with other business people or employees? Send a detailed email or memo? Walk away and forgo any money the client might pay? Sue? Or what?

DEALING WITH IMPOSSIBLE CLIENTS points up the ways in which clients can be difficult, demanding, or outright scoundrels and what to do about it. It deals with recognizing the danger signals before working with such a client or when to cut your losses to avoid further problems down the road. While the focus is on what small business owners, managers, and professionals should do, the book should also appeal to others in business with problem employees, bosses, or co-workers and those contemplating going into business for themselves.

The book begins with an introduction about how to notice warning signs to help you avoid dealing with impossible clients. Then, each chapter begins with a story about an impossible client, based on interviews with several dozen small business owners, managers, and professionals about what happened to them. Following each story, there is a discussion of what went wrong and what might have been done to prevent this. Finally, each chapter concludes with suggestions on how to deal with similar problems in your own situation, followed by a few short takeaways.

- A producer in L.A. was hired by a team to produce some commercials, so she hired and paid a team to do the shoot. Everything went very well, and the client gave her a $5800 cashiers check, which she deposited in her bank account, thinking the project had been completed successfully. But two days later she got a call from the bank, saying the cashier's check was fraudulent, so the bank was deducting the $5800 from the $12,000 in her bank account. Though the producer tried to call the client, the phone was disconnected, and presumably, the client had left town with the film in the can, never to be heard from again.

- A client kept changing his mind about what he wanted – and then blamed the graphic designer for not doing what he said to do. In the spirit of pleasing the client, the designer kept making the changes, and then faced a can't-be-pleased client, who argued that he shouldn't have to pay for all the changes, since they were the designer's mistakes. Otherwise, he wanted a full refund and would take his business elsewhere. Feeling he had already invested too much time in the project, the designer agreed not to charge for the corrections, and ironically, the final design was very close to what the designer had originally created before any changes.

In another case, I encountered a real estate "developer", who hadn't yet developed anything. But he had grandiose ideas for turning a book about big names in the field into a business, in which the book would be a small part of the company. He envisioned videos, a reality show, and he claimed endorsements from major real estate companies. Though successful real estate books average about 10,000-20,000 in sales, he imagined selling a copy of his book to almost everyone in real estate or related fields, with about 3 million in sales projected after three years. He envisioned spending about $200,000 for PR, sending the authors on a 50 city tour, and working with investors to fund a self-published book and set up a distribution deal to sell the book globally

But in the end, he turned out to be phony, since a quick Internet check revealed that some glamorous photos of luxury buildings on his site were all for show. In fact, he lived in a dumpy part of L.A. and had never developed anything. What he seemed good at was persuading people to buy into his dream and write proposals for free or give him endorsements. As a result, after I spent a few hours beginning an analysis and got an email saying I made some good points but he needed a more comprehensive report before he was willing to pay anything, I quickly bailed.

However, the experience contributed to me developing some scripts for short training videos and seminars on how to deal with workplace problems, including impossible clients. Eventually, after several more experiences with difficult clients, these encounters inspired the beginnings of this book.

PART I: AVOIDING PROBLEM CLIENTS

CHAPTER 1: AVOIDING AND TURNING DOWN IMPOSSIBLE CLIENTS

Virtually everyone experiences impossible clients, since it is often hard to tell if someone will be difficult to deal with. Just like there can be a honeymoon period in a marriage that turns into a disaster, a honeymoon can occur when one first meets a prospective client or begins working with someone. Then, over time, baggage can accumulate in any relationship, leading what starts as a good association to go bad – or hidden negative qualities can emerge, so you can find a client is not what you thought.

For instance, a client who hires you to do extensive work can turn out not to have the money to pay for the project after you are half-way through doing it. Or a client who initially seems very certain about what he wants may turn into a chameleon who keeps changing his mind and expects you to complete the job for an agreed upon price. As problems emerge in the relationship, you can use different techniques to deal with such clients and reduce the potential carnage they may do – including knowing when to walk away.

If you know how to spot potential problem clients in the first place, that can help you avoid dealing with such clients in the first place – or at least you can more firmly establish the terms under which you will work with such clients, and thereby, in effect, tame the beast. In this way, you are better able to cut down potential losses and maximize profits by weeding out bad clients and helping only the best. This is an especially important strategy, since you or your company have only a limited amount of time, and bad clients can easily become a big timewaster and drain on your resources.

Focus on the Best Clients

One strategy to avoid dealing with impossible clients is to determine who are your best clients and focus on those.

That's what Tom did in his graphic design business. He prioritized the kinds of clients he preferred to have, based on the type of work they wanted to do and the size of the job, so he could focus on clients who could best use his skills and with large enough projects to be cost-effective for himself and the client. As a result, since he was not an illustrator himself, he turned down jobs where a client wanted illustrations, rather than farming out the work to outside artists, which would mean having to supervise and vouch for someone else's work. Also, Tom turned down jobs that were too small, such as if someone asked him to design a single brochure, because he wanted larger projects with bigger companies, such as doing the graphics for a complete marketing campaign.

In this way, Tom followed the rule of prioritizing the kinds of customers a business prefers, while eliminating the clients who would take his time away from serving other more valuable customers. This approach allowed him to focus on attracting the most desirable customers representing the bulk of his business and contributing the most to his profits.

The essence of this approach is to identify the best clients for you by applying the 80-20 rule, whereby 80% of a company's business comes from 20% of its customers. Once you identify that 80%, treat those clients especially well and invest extra energy in satisfying their needs, while extending your service to them above and beyond the call of duty. They form the core or your client base, and by cultivating them, they might not only bring you more business but refer others to you. In this way, you can create even more clients who are similarly very loyal and profitable for your company. As they say, birds of a feather flock together, and you can attract even more to your flock of clients when you treat one such client very well.

Clarify What a Client Really Wants

When you first start pitching a client on working with you or begin working with a client, a good way to avoid problems down the road is to clarify what you client really wants, and make sure you can actually deliver this, so there are no unfulfilled expectations or disappointments. To this end, ask questions to get the client to indicate what the project entails, including the deliverables and the expected due date. Estimate how much time it will take you to do the different phases of the service or produce different components of the final project. This way you can set the stage for realistically fulfilling the client's expectations, which is the secret to creating customer satisfaction – and when you over-perform and over-deliver, this provides the basis for creating "raving fans" – people who love what you do and tell others about it.

For example, some questions to ask or topics to discuss and then probe further for additional details and clarification are:

- Tell me about your project. What do you want to accomplish with this?
- Who do you consider your primary audience or target market for your product or service?
- What would you like me to do to help you achieve what you want to do?
- Let's go over what specifically you would like me to do and what I can do?
- When do you want this work completed? Let's work out a time frame so I can clarify what I can do when, and when we will be meeting to discuss different phases of the project as we go along?

It's important to get this framework and timeline up front, so you know what the clients wants you to do and if it's realistic for you to do it within the parameters set up to fulfill the client's request. Additionally, once you have this framework, you can give the client a better explanation of your charges for what you will be doing. Then, whether you charge by the hour, project, completion of different elements of the project as you go along, you can explain this and work out the payment arrangements with the client. This can often be a sensitive subject, so if you have some cost guidelines to give the client, this can be helpful for the client understanding the basis of what you are charging for what.

This clarification and discussion of costs can also help you decide if you really want to work with a particular client. For example, if the client is unclear about what he or she wants or seems reluctant about your charges, saying things like "That's a lot of money?...I'll have to talk it over with my wife/husband…How can I be sure your help will really help bring me more business?...I'm not sure I need to spend this much money to achieve this result." These are all different indicates of client resistance, and even if the client decides to go ahead or soon agrees to work with you, these could be warning flags for problems ahead. For example, if the client is really straining his or her budget to work with you, even if the project will really help the client, the budget strain could lead the client to feel a kind of "client remorse," where he or she begins to find fault with everything and back away from responding to your requests for information or feedback in a timely manner, and later that resistance can lead to problems in getting paid in the future. Or the client may back out of a project after you have set aside a block of time to work with that person.

In short, know what the client really wants you to do and when and if you can do so, and if you notice any signs that the client is having doubts or second thoughts, discuss them now rather than have problems with the client later.

Look for the Warning Signs of a Bad Client

Aside from focusing on attracting the type of client you want to attract, seek to avoid prospective clients or cut your losses with current clients who might be or are difficult to deal with and are likely to be a drain on your energy. Some of these warning signs might be:

- A prospective client is an information and energy suck, who keeps calling to ask for more information and advice, essentially treating you like an unpaid consultant. But as soon as you suggest that you might set up a consulting agreement, the prospect comes back with a reason not to pay, such as saying something like: "Oh, I just had a question" or "I'm still trying to decide what to do about working together."

- A prospective client proposes to do something you consider illegal or unethical, such as setting up a business to provide a product or service without having to comply with the usual regulations or licensing for that business.

- A prospective or current client engages in any of the practices described in this book as an example of an impossible client, such as a client who keeps making mistakes or who seeks to nibble to get you to do more and more for less and less money.

- A prospective or current client who has an overbearing, arrogant, or otherwise hard-to-get along with personality, since such a client could be very emotionally draining to deal with. Some warning signs are a person who is continually complaining about other people or companies or who frequently puts other people down. In fact, you might soon find such a person becomes very critical of you, finds fault with what you do, and asks to pay less for your alleged mistakes.

- A prospective or current client who is very unclear about what he or she wants or needs and resists your efforts to help that client become clear. While it can be helpful to guide a client to develop a purpose or goals and the steps to get there, if the client seems unwilling to accept your efforts, it might be better to tell the client that he or she needs to develop that clarity before you can help and wait until the client is actually ready to proceed.

- A prospective or current client who is facing financial problems and wants you to change your usual policies to accommodate him or her. With new clients it is probably best to be firm and indicate that you can't make changes, since it can be too easy to find that the client pays others first, so you get stiffed. In dealing with current clients, it might be reasonable to offer to delay payments for a time, but then stop further work until you get paid, which provides an incentive to pay you, and you won't lose too much if the client continues to struggle and can't pay. At the same time, some clients use this approach with many businesses to get a lot of free services and then find reasons to delay or not pay. Thus, be cautious whenever the subject of lowering or delaying your usual payment comes up, since you want to focus on working with your best clients, who are the ones who regularly pay you what you are worth.

     - A prospective or current client who otherwise makes you nervous or on your guard. Sometimes you can't quite put your finger on it. But the thought of working with this client makes you uncomfortable, though you aren't sure why. In this case, it's best to trust your intuition or gut feelings; they pick up some negative vibes on an unconscious level which are telling you that this person is bad news. So if you get that warning message, it's best to listen to it and respond accordingly. It's like your survival instinct kicking in to tell you something is wrong – and if you don't listen, you may soon find out why.

     In sum, do what you can to cultivate the best clients and turn away others. If you are working with a client and you start seeing warning signs or experience gut level feelings that things aren't A-Okay, reduce your contact or cut off your relationship with that client, before you have even more problems for ignoring these signs or feelings that it's time to move on.

CHAPTER 2: HOW TO GET PROBLEM CLIENTS OUT OF YOUR LIFE

There can be many reasons why you don't ever again want to deal with a problem client and want that past or current client out of your life for good. But there could be some lingering problems in truly getting rid of that person, such as if you travel in the same social circles or if the former client thoughtlessly contacts you again to do some more work, not realizing or accepting the fact that you are determined to never work for that person again.

Here are some things you can do to deal with a client who will never go away.

- If a problem client is signed up for information on any kind of meetings or events you do, drop the client from the database.

- If a problem client has been a friend or contact on the social media, defriend the client, eliminate any following, and cut the client out of any of your databases.

- If you see a former client at a social or business event where you have mutual friends or memberships, try to avoid running into that person if possible. For instance, look away, hoping that they don't see you or don't realize that you have seen them. Or go to another part of the room or to another room.

- If you can't avoid running into that former client you want to avoid, be polite but distant and excuse yourself and move away as soon as you can. You might even use a reasonable and socially acceptable explanation, such as you have to make a call or you need to find someone at the event.

- Don't let the former client draw you into a conversation, particularly one that rehashes what happened in the past. Even if the person tries to apologize about what happened, say this isn't the time or place.

- In any personal encounter with a former client, stay calm, and don't look back to the past for explanations or excuses, which the former client may try to give you now.

- Consider that the client is completely removed from your life, and as necessary, remind yourself that this is so. If you need to feel better about this, engage in some meditation or personal ritual in which you see the client gone. Consider the relationship irrevocably severed. Remind yourself that you have completed the work you did for the client, and it is worth whatever you refunded or any extra work you did without full compensation, to have to never work with that client again.

- Once you have made this decision to no longer have anything to do with a particular client, if the client tries to call you again to do more work, graciously indicate that you think the client will be happier working with someone else. Don't try to further explanation why such an arrangement should be so, since this will just invite further discussion and attempts by the client to work with that client again. Resist any temptation to explain why you don't want to work with this client ever again.

PART II: MISTAKES AND MISINFORMATION

CHAPTER 3: WHAT TO DO WITH A CLIENT WHO MAKES MISTAKES

What should you do if you have a client who makes repeated mistakes after not following your advice, and then expects you to charge less because the client did all this extra work? That's what I experienced with a difficult client who made inspired the series of columns that led to this book. The problem began innocently enough. A client I met at one of my workshops on preparing proposals, finding agents and publishers, and publishing your own book called to say that her family wanted to publish her son's children's book. The client, I'll call Roberta, wanted me to first edit the book and then upload it to a popular self-publishing platform, CreateSpace. She said she only had enough money for part of the job, which had to be done now in time for her son's birthday, but she would have the rest in a week. So I relaxed my usual rule which most writers and editors have with individual clients of getting paid in advance for the work to be done.

At once, the series of mistakes began. First, though I was publishing their book on CreateSpace, they set up their account on Kindle. So their account name and password so I could set up their book on the site didn't work, so I initially told them what to do as I set up a book in my own account, until we discovered the mistake, and I signed on to their account.

Then, after I had edited their manuscript and inserted the pictures to appear on the right page while the text was on the left page on opening the book, the manuscript was ready to go. The son just had to check it over, make any final crops on the pictures, and either he or I could upload it.

Next came a series of mistakes and phone calls for me to help them fix their mistakes. First, their son decided to combine some of the text and photos on the same page, though he used the original unedited manuscript. Unfortunately, when his mother sent back the file for me to review, some of the photos were much larger and outside the margins. Once he fixed that and uploaded the manuscript, it was rejected because it was now below 24 pages, since he had combined the most of the text and photos on the same page. After he reinserted the photos and copy, they were reversed, so the photos were on the left and the text on the right. When I pointed that out, he redid the manuscript to correct it, but since he was working on the unedited manuscript, he had to copy and paste the edited copy into that.

After that, he was adamant he wanted to use his own cover, not a template, but he didn't follow the specs for designing a cover, so at first, he didn't have the right size or a spine, and after he corrected that, the company advised him the cover was unacceptable, because he had designed the front cover on the left and the back cover on the right like he was creating a poster, rather than a book cover where the front cover is on the right and the back cover on the left, since it folds behind the book. Though he could have made the swap himself, he hired the company's design service complete his cover.

At this point, because all his mistakes and changes resulted in more costs, Roberta called me, asking me to reduce the remaining payment I hadn't yet charged. Since I hadn't yet charged the balance, I agreed, rather than object on the grounds that all these extra costs and time were of their own making. Then, I feared, I might not get paid at all, though I had spent several extra hours helping the son fix his mistakes, due to not following my instructions or the company's specs which I pointed out to him. So I did get paid this reduced amount, although a number of other writers suggested I should have actually gotten more, because I had to spend extra time fixing their mistakes.

The experience got me thinking about what to do in the future in dealing with payments and mistakes by a client resulting in a lot of extra work and costs – and what others might do in a like situation. So here are my takeaways.

1. Get a retainer or payment in advance, and clearly indicate what this is for.

2. Explain to the client that they are welcome to make changes, but caution them about the risks of added work and costs, if they make these changes on their own.

3. Explain that if they make mistakes in making these changes, they will still be responsible for the extra time you spend to correct their mistakes.

4. Gently point out the client's mistakes, so the client recognizes them and does not think you have made them.

5. Write up guidelines about dealing with mistakes and submit them to the client before beginning the project or while doing the work, when the issue of making changes comes up.

6. Ask the client to sign or acknowledge these guidelines in an email.

CHAPTER 4: WHAT TO DO WHEN A CLIENT IS MISINFORMED AND UNWILLING TO LISTEN TO GOOD ADVICE

What should you do if you encounter a client who is misinformed and unwilling to listen to good advice? Worse, what if your efforts to advise the client result in the client becoming even more stuck in his or her position and angry about even discussing what's wrong? That's what happened to Jerry, who had an online business sending out queries for clients to professionals in various industries. To do so, he obtained mailing lists from various list brokers and cleaned them up to remove bad emails in order to use the lists with clients. Otherwise, the bounce rate would be too high, and he could soon find his service banned from sending out queries.

Since he was hoping to expand his service by adding lists in other industries, one of his prospective clients Bart proposed buying the lists together to share the costs, and then Bart planned to hire Jerry to send out his query. In turn, Jerry proposed to send out the query at a reduced rate since they would be sharing the cost of the list.

Bart accordingly bought three lists for about $200. However, after Jerry explained about the need to clean up the list before sending out a query in order to preserve his company's reputation with email service providers, Bart balked. He claimed he had found a service that would give him his own IP address and send out the queries for him, as well as remove any bounces, for only $99 a month for about 50,000 emails a month.

But when Jerry checked into the service, he discovered that it only sent out 75 queries an hour, which mean that it would take 30 days to send out a query to Bart's list of nearly 50,000 emails. Moreover, when Jerry did a test query of part of one of the lists they purchased together, he discovered and advised Bart that the bounce rate was 40%, but Bart didn't care about this warning. He even became angry when Jerry suggested that they might go back to the company and ask for a refund, because the return rate was so high. Instead, Bart justified the high rate because the list was relatively inexpensive, since a good list would be $3000 or $4000. Further, Bart told Jerry he didn't want Jerry to email him or call him about the lists they shared together, and asked Jerry to send a check for the balance of the money for the shared lists they had already gotten and another he planned to purchase for them. But given the high return rate, Jerry didn't want this additional list. However, Bart had unilaterally cut off further communication, since he was determined to do it his way, even though he had poor lists and would likely find his marketing emails not only delivered very very slowly but ultimately blocked because of the high bounce rate.

So what should Jerry have done – and what should you do if you run into a client who doesn't want to listen to your good advice – and probably may no longer be a client because of his or her attitude.

1. Don't let the experience discourage you. Not all clients will be a good fit with you.

2. Don't let this single experience cause you to hold back with other clients when you see they are making a mistake because of bad information. Continue to offer the best advice you can to other clients.

3. Do further research on the issues your client or prospective client has raised, so you are fully informed should the subject come up again.

4. When a client seeks to cut off communication because they refuse to listen to your good advice, your first reaction may be to want to call or email the person to explain or smooth over the situation. However, it's generally better not to respond under these circumstances. Instead, provide time for the person's anger to calm down – and in time, he or she is likely to find that your advice was good and he or she made a mistake in using incorrect information.

5. Think of what you might learn from the experience for the future.

6. If you still feel bad about what happened and the frayed relationship that resulted, do something to stop thinking about the situation and let it go. For example, participate in a fun activity, talk to some friends on the phone. And focus on the future, not what happened in the past.

PART III: OVERLY DEMANDING CLIENTS

CHAPTER 5: WHEN A CLIENT IS UNREASONABLE AND DEMANDING

Sometimes clients are unusually demanding and unreasonable, so when things go wrong, they seek to place the responsibility on others, far beyond what is usual. They may even, when angry, threaten to damage your reputation unless you do something to repair what happened to make up to them for something that goes beyond your own responsibility.

In law, there is a concept called "proximate damages," which means that someone is responsible for causing something if it is a likely consequence of an action, but not beyond, so someone is no longer responsible. And sometimes lawyers battle over what are the proximate results of what occurred. For example, if someone misses a train because someone gave them the wrong time for the last train and as a result walks out on the street to get a cab and gets mugged, the train is not responsible for the person getting mugged. Nor is the person who gave the person the wrong information about the train, so that he missed the last one. That's because the damage which later occurred was not a likely or foreseeable consequence of what the person providing information or the train did.

Likewise, clients sometimes lose sight of how far a person's responsibility extends, so they make unreasonable demands. You may want to show sympathy and concern and seek to calm down a client who is unreasonably angry. You might even offer some concessions to diffuse a difficult situation and keep the peace. But you also don't want to take on responsibility for something that goes beyond the scope of what you are responsible for.

That's the situation which Sidney, a motivational speaker and workshop leader faced, when he conducted a workshop on Personal Transformation for Success in his home on a residential street near the downtown of a suburban city. But when he announced the workshop through an organization he belonged to, he didn't want to give out his private address. So he asked individuals interested in the workshop to RSVP and pay the $20 fee in advance. Then, as he explained in the announcement, he would send out details on the address and directions two days before the workshop, though he indicated the general area where the workshop was located, so people could plan accordingly.

Two days before the workshop, that's exactly what he did. He sent out the location and directions to a dozen people who signed up, and a day before he sent out a second announcement. When he began the workshop, he noticed that one woman, Janet, hadn't arrived, but after waiting 15 minutes, he started his presentation, figuring she was just a no show. But three hours later, after the workshop ended, with an enthusiastic response from all the attendees, he discovered an angry email from Janet requesting a refund for the workshop, along with a tirade about how she didn't come because she got lost and spent two hours trying to find the location. As she raged:

> "I spent two hours of my Saturday attempting to find your location – nada! Asked numerous people near the intersection listed in your announcement, but no one could help me. You gave no address, and there is no signage on your location. I went home once to make sure I got the directions right and went back only to find myself at the same spot in the same quandary…I am really disappointed and this experience leads me to question the legitimacy of your group. How do new members find you?..I would like a refund for my efforts."

In response, Sidney quickly replied by email about the two emails he had sent, but Janet never got them, perhaps because her security settings didn't permit emails sent through the organization's platform. So Sidney readily refunded Janet's money and offered to send a link to a recording of the workshop to her, adding that now that he had her email, he could send her an email directly for future programs. He also said he regretted that she hadn't emailed him the night before to let him know she hadn't gotten his mailing of the location and directions, and in the future, when he announced the workshop, he would ask anyone who didn't get his mailings by the day before to let him know. Then he thought that was that. He had done what he could to make an adjustment given Janet's reason for not showing up, plus he sent a recording of the workshop at no charge.

But then he got an email from Janet saying that she thought he should do even more, since as a result of her driving around because she didn't get the directions, she had gotten into a fender bender, which would cost her several hundred dollars. So could Sidney take care of that, which she felt was the right thing for him to do under the circumstances? Otherwise, she suggested that it would be bad for his future workshops if he had dissatisfied clients. So her email implied that if he didn't cover her costs, she might bad-mouth his workshop, which was all about inspiring people to transform themselves to become successful. However, he had let her down.

But had he? The more Sidney thought about it, the more he felt her request was completely unreasonable, and even worse was her threat to damage his reputation if he didn't accede to her request. Everyone had gotten his mailing except her, and she had not let him know before the workshop that she didn't get it. So it was really his responsibility that she didn't have the correct address and spent two hours driving around, got upset, and got into an accident? Beyond giving her a refund and a recording of the event, he felt he had done all that was required. But what should he do about her anger and threat? Should he respond to try to explain why he wasn't responsible for what happened? Should he not respond at all? Ultimately, he didn't reply and didn't hear from Janet again, though he wondered if that was the best approach at the time.

What should Sidney have done to avoid this problem – and what should you do in dealing with a client is unreasonable and demanding?

1) Try at first to be understanding, sympathetic, and conciliatory, if a client has experienced problems due to their own misunderstandings or errors; but don't accept fault, responsibility, or blame in doing so.

2) Be willing to make some small concessions, if that seems reasonable to help calm the client down and make them feel better. For example, offer a refund or give the client a free book or recording that you might otherwise charge for in the spirit of good will and good customer relations. Or if the client wants a large amount, say over $50 or $100, offer that as a credit on a future program.

3) Keep in mind the legal concept of proximate causation in assessing whether you are responsible for what happened to the client as a result of something the client did, such as getting lost in trying to find your meeting place or workshop, since they got the directions wrong or didn't get them, and didn't tell you in advance that they didn't receive them. If something untoward happens to the client, such as falling in a ditch, getting mugged, or getting into a car accident, you are not responsible, since that event was not a foreseeable result of anything you did or did not do.

4) If a client makes any threats about what he or she will do if you don't satisfy their unreasonable demands, just do what is reasonable under the circumstances to avoid any potential for harm and calm down the client. For example, if the client is responding with a kind of "road rage," it's best to back down and get away from the encounter. You shouldn't try to explain or reason with someone who is being irrational, since they won't listen. Or try a delaying tactic to offer to talk about the situation later, when the client has calmed down. Under the circumstances, the best conflict resolution techniques are avoidance and delay; avoid any confrontational technique which is likely to escalate the situation; and you have to diffuse any negative emotions before you can use the two other common conflict resolution techniques of compromise or collaboration to find a win-win resolution.

5) Recognize that the client is making any unreasonable threats out of anger, which often arises from self-blame directed

34

outward, since the person doesn't want to accept that the fault lies within him or herself. But afterwards, in most cases, once the client calms down and reason takes over, the client won't carry out the threat and will often go away or come back being very apologetic for his or her bad behavior.

6) If a former client does attempt to carry out any threat, such as trying to ruin your reputation to get revenge or retaliate in some other way, you might have the basis for claims against the client, such as for defamation or even for criminal charges. In this case, sometimes a warning to the former client about the consequences might be enough to end any retaliation, and the person will simply disappear, never to be heard from again.

CHAPTER 6: WHEN A CLIENT DOESN'T RESPECT YOUR TIME

A big problem for many professionals is what to do about a client who doesn't respect your time. This lack of respect can take various forms. A client is repeatedly late, gives an excuse each time, and expects you to provide the same service as you would if he or she was on time, though you might have other clients scheduled for the next time slot. Another client might schedule appointments, but then call to cancel or reschedule some appointments at the last minute – or sometimes the client doesn't show and calls to apologize later. Then, there is the client who tries to gain more time during a consultation session or meeting with you without paying any more, usually by raising more questions to discuss at the end of the meeting.

Alicia, who worked as a massage therapist, energy worker, and fitness coach had these problems with some clients who came to her for massages, energy assessments, and coaching on becoming more healthy and fit. Unfortunately, she tried to be too nice and accommodating to some clients and felt they took advantage of her. But she feared if she tried to be more firm about her time, she might lose some of these clients and she needed the income.

For example, one client, Tom, was a successful businessman who owned his own company and frequently traveled to go to business meetings and to make pitches for new business. Thus, when he came to see her about every two weeks for a massage, he wanted to chill out and relax for an hour or two, in order to recharge his energy to go into his next weeks of meetings. And often his secretary set up the appointments with Alicia, so it wasn't always clear whether Tom knew about and was available for these appointments.

Another client, Suzanne, was a conscientious middle-class mother with several school age kids, and she spent much of her time ferrying her kids to multiple classes. Sometimes she had to deal with unexpected emergencies, such as a child having an accident or fighting with another kid at school, so she had to see the nurse or vice-principle about the problem. Thus, due to these unpredictable situations, Suzanne was often late, gasping for breath as she ran in the door, after which she explained the latest crisis she had to deal with. "I'm so sorry to be late," she would conclude apologetically each time. But then Suzanne expected Alicia to give her the usual full hour or close to that, which work if Alicia didn't have another client for the next hour. If so, Alicia had to explain that she had to Suzanne a shorter than usual session, which usually led to Suzanne becoming angry, so sometimes she tried to ask the next client to come a little later, if she could reach him or her phone or email, or occasionally she ask the client to wait a short time if he or she came on time. However, all of these situations left Alicia feeling uncomfortable and feeling disrespected by Suzanne's self-centered, cavalier behavior.

Finally, there was Joe, who always had a pressing issue to raise at the end of a session, and usually he would introduce the issue by saying: "I just need a few more minutes," although the discussion would normally go longer. In some cases this meant Joe had to ask a client in the waiting room to wait a few minutes or he had to awkwardly try to end a conversation with Joe, because of the waiting client. But at other times, when no one was waiting, Joe seemed to think it was fine to continue the discussion for an extra 10 to 20 minutes, though he didn't want to pay anymore.

What should Alicia have done to avoid this problem – and what should you do in dealing with a client who doesn't respect your time?

The basic way to deal with this kind of problem is to set up policies about how you are providing your time to clients and let your clients know in advance. With new clients, you can readily provide these guidelines when you first start working together, and it can work well for you or a staffer to explain these policies at a first meeting – and then provide the client with a written description of these guidelines. This way it is very clear what you expect. If you have worked with clients in the past, you can discuss how you plan to handle scheduling in the future, provide a short grace period of about a month, and then initiate your new policy. If clients aren't willing to respect these policies, it may be best to let them go and find new clients who do respect your time.

Certainly allow for exceptions in the case of true emergencies, and perhaps be more flexible the first month you work with a client or have established new policies with old clients. Then, be ready to enforce these policies or say goodbye to clients who won't go along you're your new arrangements.

An example of how these policies might work is the approach used by Jim, a dentist with a very active practice. He has a policy whereby a client who has to cancel or reschedule an appointment within 24 hours will be charged for that time; and if the client cancels or reschedules from 24 to 48 hours, he or she will be charged half. After that, there is no charge, although a client who repeatedly cancels or reschedules appointments will be charged the full amount after the third time. However, any fees will be waived for a first time client or in case of a true emergency, such as a medical crisis, but not for a client going on a business trip or meeting a client. Jim found the approach worked very well by reducing the number of appointments rescheduled and cancelled, which used to drive his staff crazy, since they had to get on the phones to invite clients with later appoints to come sooner. In addition, this policy provided extra income from repeat offenders who wanted to continue to see Jim, because they valued his work.

You can readily change the specifics of when to charge for a canceled or changed appointment. At least have some specific consequence in place to compensate for cancellations and changes, and put clients on notice of whatever arrangements you choose.

As for clients who come late and want the full amount of time scheduled or clients who want to push their time a little longer, have a policy to deal with those situations, and explain it to new and old clients, and prepare written guidelines. For example, one counselor who does this is Marianne. She makes it very clear to clients that the time scheduled is their hour, and if they are late, she will usually have to give them less time, because she has another client booked, and she can't push back all her clients to a later time. If she did, they would have to wait and may have other appointments after hers, so any change would be unfair to them. Should a client running late feel he or she won't have enough time, the client can always cancel or reschedule (and then any policies for making changes will apply). Likewise, if on-time clients want more time, Marianne explains about her policy of starting with her client for the next time slot on time. If she doesn't have a waiting client, she explains that she could continue the session for an additional fee, if the client agrees to pay it, which most do, or if they don't want to pay, they can leave now. Likewise, you can create a similar type of policy governing what to do when clients come late or want more time.

In short, set up policies about managing your time and let your clients know what they are. Provide some flexibility in the first few weeks to give clients the benefit of the doubt when they have problems adjusting to your current time schedule. Otherwise, consider this approach one of setting boundaries – though instead of boundaries on space, these are boundaries on access to your time. Establishing these boundaries is like you are creating a gate with certain requirements for clients to get in. Then, once they are there for that time, you can give them your full attention. But if they don't accept these arrangements, they can't get in, whether new or old clients. At times, you may be willing to open the gate or get an extra toll; just make it clear to clients that these policies about operating the gate and deciding what clients to let in under what conditions are up to you.

CHAPTER 7: WHEN A PROSPECTIVE CLIENT TAKES ADVANTAGE OF YOUR FREE INTRODUCTORY OFFER

Providing a free sampling of what you do can be a way to drum up new business, so often individual professionals or companies make this offer. It can take various forms. A free introductory consultation for 20 or 30 minutes to an hour. A free copy of a book by a professional consultant. A free session using the equipment in a gym. A day to try out a new software program. A coupon for something for free. A trial subscription for a few days, a week, or a month. Or an offer might be for an informational discussion and a hands-on demonstration of how the equipment works. Whatever the offer, the idea is to get the person to try out your product and service, like it, and want more.

But sometimes you may encounter a prospective client who is trying to take advantage of you by using your free service or program, but from the outset, is clearly not interested in even considering your offer. He or she is just interested in the free part, and isn't interested in hearing any more about how you might help them with your product or service in the future.

That's what happened for Dan, a fitness trainer and coach, who worked at a gym that offered a variety of workout equipment for building strength, cardio, endurance, and other abilities. While many clients of the gym only came to use the facility, some were interested in working with a trainer who could guide them in creating a fitness program based on best developing their physical abilities and compensating for any current weaknesses, disabilities, or injuries.

Dan hoped to build his clientele who were interested in working with a trainer, and he posted his profile on various sites, along with a complimentary introduction in a one-hour session. One man who saw his posting was Victor, who had previously taken a number of classes in a variety of disciplines, including boxing, yoga, Zumba, and aerobics, although he had never had a personal training session. But while he was curious about what a personal trainer did, he was more interested in a brief introduction and then using most of the time to work out. However, when he called to set up a session and asked Dan how much time would be spent in talking and in working out, Dan explained there would be about 40-50 minutes of conversation and about 10-20 minutes of exercise. When Victor balked at this much time for discussion, since he considered himself already physically fit, Dan agreed to limit the discussion to about 20 minutes followed by a 40 minute workout.

Thus, when Victor arrived, Dan shortened his usual explanation about how working with a trainer had helped himself, how he would help his clients determine the best exercises for them, and how he worked with his clients on a weekly basis to develop a long-term program that he would adapt to them as they became more fit. But after 15 minutes, Victor was clearly getting restless. He seemed to be tuning Dan out, as he looked towards the gym where several other people were already working out. Dan was aware of Victor's lack of attention, and was about to wrap up his presentation, when Victor became abusive and disrespectful, telling him: "Look, why don't you stop talking. I've heard enough to know what you do. So why don't you take me over to the machines and let me work out now?"

Reluctantly, Dan took Victor over to the treadmill, and when he started to explain about how Victor could adjust the tilt and speed, Victor shot back: "Listen, I already know this. You haven't told me anything I don't already know. So why don't you just let me work out?"

At this point, Dan could barely contain his anger and shot back: "Look, if you're not happy with what I've been telling you, you can just leave." At first, Victor glared at him silently, as Dan watched him nervously, not sure what he might do. But then, Victor simply got up and announced: "This has been a total waste of time, and I didn't even get to work out." Then, he left, and Dan sighed with relief, thinking that was that. However, the following day, Victor posted a long screed against Dan on one of the popular business review sites, complaining about how Dan wasted his time by trying to discuss his training program, when he mostly wanted to work out by trying out new equipment.

Dan tried to temper the 1 star review by saying he was sorry that Victor had a bad experience, and reaffirmed that he was clear in explaining the reason he was offering a complimentary session: "to provide a learning environment for the curious," and "to provide a baseline for a potential new client." He pointed out that on the phone he had clearly explained the intent of the session, which was not just to provide a "free" workout, but to also be educational, since everyone has "form issues" and "everyone can use a coach's eye to aid in the process." Unfortunately, his explanation only gave Victor a platform to further denigrate Dan's training program and restate that he didn't want to listen to the owner talk about his training program, which he felt was a waste of time, since he was already physically fit and just wanted to work out and didn't want to waste time in non-physical activity. Perhaps from this workout he might see if the trainer's coaching might have some value to him, but otherwise, he just wanted to work out.

Thus, clearly, from the outset, Dan and Victor were not on the same page as to what they hoped to gain from the free complimentary session.

What should Dan have done to avoid this problem – and what should you do in dealing with a prospective client who responds to an offer for a free introductory product or service, but isn't really interested in a future service with you beyond the free offer?

1) Make it very clear in advance what you are offering, and if a prospective client tries to change this, such as being mainly interested in using the equipment or software, rather than listening to you talk about how you might help in future sessions, it doesn't seem like this is a good potential client. Consider including in your initial announcement of the offer a sentence to explain that this offer is only for those who might benefit from your service, which will be determined through a preliminary phone

conversation to those who want to sign-up for this complimentary offer.

2) Remind the prospective client that the purpose of the session is to see if there is a good fit between you and the client; if not, this sessions would not be useful for the person.

3) Clarify if there is a good fit between you and the prospective client by asking some baseline questions about that person to see if there is a match between the type of clients you have helped in the past and what this person wants for the future.

4) If the prospective client doesn't have the characteristics or interests of the people you have typically worked with, ask more questions in your initial phone conversation to probe further about what that person needs or wants. If you don't feel that you may be able to fulfill those needs, indicate that on the phone to give the prospect a chance to correct your assessment and show that he or she would really like to consider your offer to help.

5) If after extensive explanation and probing, you feel this person is not likely to want to use your products or services beyond getting a free trial, discourage this person from taking your free offer, and tell the person that you don't think he or she would benefit.

6) If the prospective client should become confrontational or abusive when you explain how you can help, back off, and as long as it is safe, let the person go ahead and do what he wants to try out the product or service, without providing further information about how you can help. It would seem clear that this person is not going to purchase your products or services, and you can diffuse the situation by backing off.

7) If the prospective client insults you or is disrespectful, try to tune that person out and don't respond or respond minimally. That way you can stay calm and relaxed and not let the person's comments get to you, so you become upset or try to argue back. Your goal should be to get the client to leave as soon as possible and not try to respond in kind, which might only lead to an escalating war of words.

8) Should the prospective client later post a negative review about your product or service, don't try to respond directly, which might only encourage the client to repeat, perhaps in even more detail and with more invective, his or her complaints against you. Rather, find a few people who have used your product or service and have had a very positive experience to write a few reviews for you. These new reviews will go to the top of the list as more recent reviews, so his review will drop back and have less and less influence on prospective clients, the more you get positive reviews.

PART IV: CAUGHT IN THE BLAME GAME

CHAPTER 8: WHEN A CLIENT IS NEGATIVE AND COMPLAINS ABOUT EVERYTHING

Some people have a negative attitude and complain about everything, which can be a real downer. Sometimes they may be overly demanding and quick to complain about something you are doing, but they keep returning to work with you, so you know they must like your work – at least for the most part, when they don't find something to find fault with. But primarily the problem in working with them is they use you as a sounding board to complain about what is happening in their life and what is going on in the world. So you can end up feeling drained and depressed after dealing with such clients, because they are like a sponge, taking away your good feelings and leaving you feeling blue, until you can soak up some more positive energy from doing something else.

That's the experience which Natalie, a hair stylist and beauty salon operator, had in working with Debra, who was a clerk and receptionist for a lawyer specializing in estates and trusts. So Debra's negative attitude seemed a good fit for where she was working, since the typical clients were people towards the end of their life and their families, who were preparing documents on what to do with the dying person's assets after their death. The other typical clients were bereaved widows and children seeking counsel on how to implement the will of their dearly departed. Or the clients might be angry family members and relatives asking what to do if there wasn't a will or seeking to contest a will if they didn't get enough. Debra spoke to them while they waited in the reception area to talk to the lawyer, and she was a good listener, since she enjoyed hearing tales of misery and mistrust.

When Natalie worked on cutting and styling her hair every few weeks, Debra was only too eager to report on the complaints of the law firm's clients, as well as her own. Frequently she told Natalie: "No, you're doing it wrong again. Just look at the picture I brought and cut my hair like that. Not too long and not too short over my ears. You always start to cut too much, so I have to keep reminding you so you do it right." As usual, Natalie listened silently and cut Debra's hair as she usually did, since it seemed like Debra just wanted to complain even before she cut anything, though she knew what to do from previous visits.

But even more annoying was Debra's litany of complaints about anything and everything for about 20 minutes. It was as if Debra was using her monthly appointments as a soapbox, where she could freely talk about all the things she found fault with, including things she had complained about before. For example, she repeatedly complained about how her children who had their own families and lived in other parts of the state didn't come to visit on holidays or school vacations, saying they had to work or had other prior commitments. But they owed her at least one visit a year, she complained, and they didn't ask her to visit them because they said they didn't have enough room for her to stay with them, and it was too expensive for her to stay in a motel. Plus Debra complained about the rise in crime in the city; about the poor roads near her house that the city hadn't fixed; about the noise from neighbors' parties, and the failure of the police to come when she called them; and besides, the neighbors should have invited her, and then she wouldn't complain. The complaints went on and on, except when Debra couldn't say anything because she was under a hair dryer after a hair coloring for about 20 minutes while Natalie worked on another customer.

At the end of the day, Natalie felt exhausted by listening to Debra's tirade. Though she thought about telling Debra she couldn't come to her salon anymore, she felt she needed the money. So what should Natalie do to avoid this problem – and what should you do in dealing with a client who is so negative about everything that he or she gets you down?

1) If appropriate, ask the client not to talk about things that are negative about others by explaining that this is distracting you from your work, and you want to do a good job.

2) If the client is saying something negative about what you are doing or will do, just acknowledge hearing the comment, and carry on to do your usual good job.

3) Remind yourself that the client has a negative personality, and you should not take any negative criticisms of yourself personally.

4) Shield yourself psychologically from this negativity, so it doesn't affect you. For example, imagine you have a shield of white light surrounding you and pushing away any negative thoughts and feelings. Or tune out the negative comments, so you barely hear them or don't hear them at all, as if they are very far away.

5) Think of the opposite of what the person is saying and respond accordingly. For example, if the person says something bad about an organization, individual, or company, say something good. If the person complains about something their city is doing, describe how you heard about the city's great new program. If the person responds by becoming quiet or being less negative in their next comments, great – this approach is working. Or if the person responds with more negative or argumentative comments, go back to another strategy, so you tune that person out or put a psychological shield around you.

6) If all else fails, consider dropping this person as a client if you can afford to do so – and look for another client you can work with instead. Remember that you can always drop a client if the arrangement isn't working for you. If appropriate, explain why you are dropping the client – and if the person complains about being dropped, stay firm unless the client offers to change, and then agree to make another attempt to work with the client on a trial basis. But if it still doesn't work, that's it. Clearly tell the client you can't continue to work with that person anymore.

CHAPTER 9: WHAT TO DO WHEN CLIENTS WANT YOU TO TAKE THE BLAME

Sometimes clients ignore your advice or are so rushed that they move ahead on something, even when you caution them to wait. They are so concerned with making a deadline, even though they don't have to or are accepting exceptionally high risks to take advantage of a special opportunity. Then, when things go south, they want you to take the blame, because you didn't stop them from doing what they were determined to do, so they ignored your advice. The same situation might occur if they ignore your advice and act for any other reason.

That's what happened to Raymond, a financial adviser and broker, after an article appeared in the newspaper about a new start-up company in the biomedical field with a seemingly strong, well-connected team. The company was issuing its first stock offering, and his clients, a middle-aged couple, Mr. and Mrs. Paulson, wanted to get involved. They discussed the investment with their kids, who lived nearby with their own families, and they all decided it would be a great opportunity to get in on the ground floor and gain high profits when the company went public.

However, Raymond had some concerns when he looked into the company. Its success was dependent on a yet unproven technology, and he urged the couple to be cautious, because they were approaching their retirement years. He advised them that this would be a risky investment for anyone who didn't already have a substantial amount of capital and could afford to lose it.

But still the Paulsons were insistent on making a substantial investment. They even cited the opinion of one of their relatives who was a successful day trader as evidence that Raymond's approach was holding them back. Thus, against his better judgment, Raymond made the transaction for them. He even spent extra time on the phone with them to help them with the necessary paperwork, as well as advising them on how to transfer their more conservative but less lucrative investments into the new investment.

After that for a few weeks, their stock in the new company performed very well, and they thanked Raymond for finally going along with them, so they could buy the stock at a very low price, rather than them to spend a few days to find another broker and lose some profit as a result.

But then, what Raymond had concerns about happened. A report came out showing that the company's new medical technology had encountered some difficulties in its trials, so it didn't get the expected approvals. In fact, some early users in the trials had negative reactions and were even threatening to sue the company. So within days the stock went down, down, and down.

When Mr. Paulson called him frantically about what to do, Raymond told them to sell as quickly as possible to cut down their losses to get back about two-thirds of what they invested, rather than potentially losing much more. So they did that. But afterwards, they sought to blame Raymond. Though he told them he had advised them against investing in the stock in the first place, they now claimed he didn't do enough to stop them from investing in it. They said he should have done extensive research on the stock, which he didn't, though he tried to explain that he didn't do this research, since they were insistent they wanted to invest in the stock right now while it was at its lowest point.

That didn't matter, they argued, insisting he was still to blame, because he had handled the transaction that caused their loss. So now they wanted him to make up the money they lost, and they even implied that if he didn't do so, they would tell others negative things about him. "Getting a bad recommendation is like getting 500 good ones," Mrs. Paulson said, and then she further appealed to him on the grounds that "You should do the right thing, because it's the right thing to do," and because they considered him a "good person." Otherwise, they would change their opinion of him, and other people they knew who were considering investing with him might decide not to hire him as their broker.

So what should Raymond have done to avoid this problem – and what should you do in dealing with a client who continues to insist that you should take the blame for their errors and additionally pay them back for their losses?

1) Tell the client that you can't do what he or she wants, because you feel the client is rushing into something that you don't think the client should do until you have time to check it out, and you don't want to aid the client in making a mistake.

2) Before you agree to do what the client wants, write up a letter for the client to sign, indicating that you are performing as the client wishes against your advice, and that the client agrees to take responsibility if the outcome isn't what the client wants.

3) When the client contacts you to get you to take the blame, send the client a letter in writing using email or certified mail in which you point out why you are not to blame, because you cautioned the client in advance and the client insisted on doing what they did against your advice. So you are not to blame for what subsequently occurred, after the client did what they wanted to do.

4) Don't let the client's warning of a bad recommendation lead you to agree to a client's unwarranted claim for compensation, especially when a significant amount of money is involved. In a small case, it might be worth a refund of a few hundred dollars to get the client to go away and not bad mouth you. But if the client is seeking thousands of dollars by blaming you for something which you didn't do wrong, don't let the client bully you. Often such a client won't follow-through, and if they make any false claims about you, they will commonly only tell a small circle of associates. If their criticism goes any further, you have a basis for a defamation suit against them, and you can warn them of the consequences if they share their negative criticism with others.

5) Ignore the client's appeals for you to do the "right thing" or do what your conscience tells you to do, since the client is just trying to guilt trip you, rather than acknowledging the client's own mistakes. The "right thing" would actually be for the client to recognize his or her own error.

CHAPTER 10: WHAT TO DO WHEN CLIENTS WRONGLY FIND FAULT WITH YOUR WORK OR CHANGE WHAT THEY WANT

Sometimes clients change their minds about what they want and then try to wrongly find fault with your work. This can be a more difficult problem for individuals who have recently started their business, so they can't point to the references and credentials of working with a long string of past clients to show that they know what they are doing and the client is wrong or that the original work is better than what the client wants now.

That's what happened to Dennis, a videographer who was doing promotional video for clients. He had one client, Vernon, a family therapist, who had written a book on resolving conflicts in the family and wanted to create a video to promote this book, which he was publishing himself. He told Dennis that he had a limited budget, and he hired Dennis for that reason, since his rates were about a third of what long-time video production companies charged. So he was paying just $1500 rather than $4000-5000 from an established company.

Soon after hiring Dennis, Vernon signed a contract indicating that Dennis would be making a 2-3 minute video for him, with a third down, a third at the film shoot, and the final payment after editing was completed. To produce the video, Dennis got a small team together – a writer who worked out the script with Vernon, a man to handle sound, a third team member to set up lights, and an editor for the post-production work.

The day of the shoot, the team set up a black screen for the background, posed Vernon in front of it, and Dennis took a series of shots with different poses, along with some close-ups of the book, so these could later be edited in, as Dennis talked about his book. Plus Vernon provided some video of himself leading groups with families, though the video was obviously shot by an amateur, since it was too bright, slightly out of focus, and jerky.

At the end of the film shoot, which lasted about three hours, not the two hours specified in the agreement, since Dennis wanted to have plenty of footage for the editor to choose from, Vernon seemed very happy. "Good job," he said, and he told Dennis to go ahead and charge the second payment.

But after the editing was nearly completed, and Julie, the editor, sent him a rough for his comments before rendering a high resolution final, Vernon suddenly found fault with the video because he "looked too old" But that's the way he looked, Dennis argued. Then, the team should have used make-up to make him look younger, Vernon said. Moreover, he now claimed the lighting was too bright, which showed off the bags under his eyes, so the lighting should have been more subdued and diffused. Moreover, though he had gone back and forth with the writer on the script, he now said there were important things he wanted to say that were left out during the filming. And he should have been filmed holding his book, though he could have easily asked to set up such a shot during their three hour session. Further, he complained that his video of the group sessions should have been used, though Dennis pointed out that it was so badly filmed that it would undermine his professionalism.

The debate went on and on, and Julie did what she could to soften Vernon's look with a diffusion lens, while adding in some clips from his home video. But in the end, Vernon refused to pay the final payment and filed a claim with his credit card company to get all of the money he charged back, though ironically, the new video production company he hired used almost exactly the same set up with a black screen and the same lighting, so he looked just as old as before. Subsequently, he did lose his claim to get back his initial payments, and Dennis and his team split up the payments they did get, so everyone at least got a partial payment for their work.

So what should Dennis have done to avoid this problem – and what should you do in dealing with a client who wrongly finds fault your work?

1) Show the client examples of previous work you have done to indicate the different styles used and ask the client to indicate which style he or she would like.

2) Explain carefully in the beginning when you work with a client what all the usual steps will be. Ask if the client fully understands what you will be doing and if the client wants anything else added. Then, write up a description of what you or other team members will do at each phase of the process, and get the client to sign this before your proceed with any work.

3) As you develop any phase of the project, such as writing a script, selecting a style, or choosing a background, ask for the client's input and approvals. Should the client want to include any work that isn't professionally done, explain your reasons for not planning to include it. If the client insists, ask the client to sign a waiver describing what he or she wants you to do, though it is against your professional advice.

4) If you are doing any design or production work for the client, provide the client with preliminary sketches or show the client some initial video takes to get the client's go-ahead.

5) Get a final payment – or most of the final payment, say less 10% -- before you complete the project. This way you are paid as you go along for all or most of the work before completing it.

6) As possible, get the client to pay you for the different phases of the project with a check, since you not only don't pay merchant fees but it is harder for a client to get a refund when there is a dispute about the quality of the work. The client has to take any dispute paid by check to court, whereas a client can easily make a credit card or PayPal claim. Should there be such a claim, even if you win, you have the hassle of providing a written defense to claims of unacceptable work. Or if the client knows to file a claim of fraud, the client is likely to prevail just for claiming that, since in a fraud case, the client has the benefit of the doubt and is more likely to have a fraud charge accepted, even if it is false and you have plenty of evidence to show you did the work.

PART V: PAYMENT PROBLEMS

CHAPTER 11: WHAT TO DO WHEN A CLIENT TRIES TO NIBBLE TO GET MORE FOR LESS

What should you do if you think you have wrapped up a deal with a client for a certain amount, but then the client asks for a series of extras – usually over a period of time rather than all at once? This is why it's called a nibble, because it's like take a series of small bites of something. Real estate people frequently encounter such a client, when they think they are about to close on a sale. The client starts asking for add-ons, such as can the owner fix the roof; can the owner cover the cost of a paint-job; can the owner leave the bookcases in the den? And so on and on, and often owners agree rather than stop a sale of several hundred thousand dollars over a few thousand dollars more in extras given to the owner.

Such nibbles go on all the time in business, whether you are selling a property or business to your providing professional services. Clients seek to get as much as they can for as little money as possible, and may keep on asking even after you reach what you think is an agreement. They still ask for more, often over a few days or weeks, as add-ons to a hoped for sale, and frequently sellers or service providers give in, thinking this will close the current sale as well as encourage more business in the future. But is that something you really want to do?

That's what happened to Frank, who helped clients in writing their books. He made arrangements with one client, Nathan, which turned into something of a nightmare, because Nathan was co-writing the book with another person who was paying the bills. So at one point, Nathan had trouble getting his partner to pay in a timely manner, so he asked Frank if he could keep writing to make their deadline. Because the book was on a timely subject in the news, Frank made an exception to getting payment upfront for work to do, since Nathan kept assuring him they had a contract and he would be paid. So Frank caved, concerned the project would end and he wouldn't get paid at all. Eventually, he was paid, but there was a three month delay, and in the meantime, Nathan kept adding in some extra services, such as a last minute chapter of about 25 pages beyond the original contract word. Also, Nathan asked Frank to write up information from some online articles and to meet with him to do some interviews for the book. As a result of these requests, Frank spent about 30 hours more than estimated to complete the project. And, of course, Nathan didn't pay anymore.

Then, Nathan contacted Frank about another book. This time he promised to pay all in advance and pay more if the word count went over, plus he added in a few thousand dollars for editing. So Frank agreed on the amount and terms. But soon after Nathan advised Frank that he would be sending a substantial payment up front in a few weeks, he explained how he would also send Frank topics to research for the chapters he would be writing. Further, he said he planned to come to Frank's city for a couple of days, so they could do some interviews. Oh, and then the editing would be for about 25,000 words that Nathan had written himself, whereas Frank had understood this fee for editing for what he had already written to polish it up. Thus, even though Nathan had corrected for previous problems and an extra word count, now Frank felt that Nathan was asking more still extra work, though the particular type of work was different.

So what should Fred do, and what should you do in a similar situation with a client who asks for more and more regardless of your industry?

1. Remember that no written agreement is binding until all parties sign it, and you can always void or change an informal agreement to be followed up by a written agreement. Just don't take any money for an agreement until you are sure you want to do it.

2. Remind yourself that it can be better not to take on a project if you will be making substantially less than your usual per hourly rate, after you figure out the number of hours you are likely

to spend for that income, and include any of your costs, such as for travel.

3. Factor in the amount of time or any costs involved in doing any extra work that the client is requesting, and assess how much that extra work will impact your earnings for doing the project. Also, consider the likelihood of getting one or more other clients to replace the work for this client and how much you need the income from that client, even if less than your usual hourly earnings.

4. Based on your assessment of likely earnings, likely alternate clients, and your need for income now, decide on whether you want to accept what the client is requesting. If not, ask for more money or doing less of the extra work requested. In other words, be prepared to accept the agreement as is, negotiate, or say no to any extras.

5. Diplomatically explain to the client how what he or she is asking goes beyond the original scope of the project. Then, discuss various alternatives – the client can pay more; the client can ask for less based on prioritizing what is more or less important; or the client can propose other possibilities.

6. If the client is reasonable and realistic, you can generally work out an understanding. But be prepared if the client is unwilling to make any changes in what he or she is demanding. If so, it may be best to indicate that you can't take on the project, because it will involve too much extra work without compensation; and be ready to walk away. Sometimes this ultimatum may be enough to get the client to agree to your last proposed terms or even come back with a reasonable counter-offer. If not, explain you regretfully can't take on this project at this time and walk away.

In short, recognize when a client is trying to nibble you down to get more for less – and be ready to negotiate for more. Then, turn down an unacceptable arrangement, unless you need to make an exception because you are experiencing a slow-down, and really need the income though it's less than you would normally make for doing that work.

CHAPTER 12: WHEN TO GIVE CLIENTS A REFUND TO GET THEM OUT OF YOUR LIFE

Sometimes clients are so needy and impossible to deal with that it's better to give them a refund even after you have done the work for them, so they will go away, not file a frivolous complaint, or bad mouth you to other clients, even though they are in the wrong. Sometimes it's not worth the hassle of trying to explain your position, especially when the amount involved is very small.

That's what happened to Simon, a graphic designer, who had spent about six hours working for a client, Tamara, who had a rush job for her son but kept changing her mind about what he wanted for a an animated video. She came with her husband and son to one of the workshops Simon gave on using various graphic programs to create short videos.

A few weeks after the workshop, Tamara contacted Simon about helping her son Andre create an animated video and explained that she wanted everything done in time for her son's birthday. Because she had been to his workshop, Simon pushed aside some other projects, as well as gave her a discount on his work of helping Andre use one of the programs, charging her $500, instead of $600.

To speed up the process, he uploaded some of Andrea's illustrations along with some short copy, so the copy would be on one screen and the illustration on the next screen. But after Simon completed the video and sent it back to Tamara for a final approval, Andre decided he wanted to make some changes, and some illustrations ended up on the wrong screens or the copy ended up on top of the illustrations. One of Andre's designs even had embedded copy with errors. Also, the music they selected was too short and ended before the video did, so Simon had to help Tamara select new music.

After that, Simon experienced anxious phone calls back and forth with Tamara for several hours until about 2 a.m. as he helped her fix errors her son had made. After each call, Tamara thanked Simon profusely for all his help. Finally, it seemed the video was done in time for Andre's birthday dinner the next day. So Simon guided them through the process of setting up their account and uploading their final video. But the next day, Tamara called to say they had to spend more time making additional adjustments, because Andre wanted to substitute another illustration, and now they had to pay the company to make this substitution. So would Simon give them a reduction to $400, because they spent all this extra time and had to pay the company the extra amount? Grudgingly, Simon agreed, just to settle the matter, although their repeated changes had led to more work for him.

But the matter wasn't settled, since a month later, Tamara called him back. This time, she complained that some people who bought the video reported that there were errors in the copy and some illustrations were in the wrong place. So now she wanted Simon to give her a refund of another $200. Though Simon explained that the video was ready to go before her son began making changes, that she approved everything after several hours of conversations, and that she wanted the video uploaded right away for her son's birthday, Tamara argued that as a professional he should have caught the mistakes. Then, she argued that he should do the right thing by her and that if she had bad things to say about him that could hurt his business, adding with some irony that if he made this adjustment, she hoped to have future projects for him to work on.

At this point, Simon just wanted Tamara and her family to go away, and he offered a $100 refund if that would that resolve everything. "No, $150," she said. At last, she agreed to a $125 refund, but had one more request. Would Simon look at the final video her son created and say what he thought, if she sent him a link. "Sure," he agreed and quickly refunded the charge, relieved that ending any arrangement with Tamara was well worth earning $275 for what should have been $900 for his work. He even banned Tamara and her family from signing up for future workshops, so he would never have to deal with them again.

What should Simon have done to avoid this problem – and what should you do in dealing with a client who keeps blaming you for their errors and wants to pay you less?

1) Don't agree to do a rush job if you don't have the time to carefully check the work. Or explain very clearly to the client the risks of rushing through a creative project, where you don't have time to do your normal quality control.

2) If your client still wants you to do a rush job, get a signed agreement in which the client acknowledges that this is a rush job and agrees to pay you for your time. Further, the client should recognize and agrees to any corners you have to cut to make the rush deadline.

3) If the client asks for reductions in what you are charging, because the client is creating more work for him or herself and claims a financial hardship to pay what you have charged, agree to a refund. Additionally, ask the client to sign a written understanding that he or she accepts this reduced amount in full payment for the work.

4) If the client tries to hold you responsible for problems in the work that led the client to do extra work, don't accept any blame for the client's extra work or losses. Recognize that sometimes clients seek to blame others so they will feel better about what happened, rather than recognizing that they at fault; also accepting blame can open you up to further demands for a refund. To make sure there is no misunderstanding, send the client a letter by email or mail explaining how you did what the client wanted to meet a rush deadline and that any mistakes which you corrected were due to what the client did.

4) If the client continues to ask for further reductions and pleads a low income, especially if this is a relatively small amount, say under $200, agree to this reduction with the understanding that this will end the relationship with the client.

5) If the client has paid by a credit card or PayPal, quickly refund the money. If you have gotten paid by check, quickly send

the client back your own check, and note on the back that this refund represents a full refund pre your agreement with the client.

6) Stay calm, even if the client starts getting emotional or crying. You have to act like the adult, when your client is behaving irrationally and making false claims about what your client believes you have done wrong what happened is really your client's mistake.

7) While you can outwardly sympathize with the client to be diplomatic, don't try to see things from the client's perspective, since the client doesn't correctly understand the situation and won't accept responsibility for his or her errors.

PART VI: UNETHICAL AND CROOKED CLIENTS

CHAPTER 13: WHAT TO DO WHEN A CLIENT IS DISHONEST

What should you do if you encounter a client who lies, cheats, and eventually steals from you? That's what happened to Cynthia, who provided various marketing and PR services to a client I'll call Derrick, to protect the identity of the innocent and guilty.

Derrick initially approached Cynthia to help him create a marketing and promotional campaign for his busines44s as a CPA and financial adviser. He was finding his business slowing down, because there was growing competition from large firms which provided the same services under a branded corporate name. He needed to do something to stand out and emphasize his more personal touch in independent practice, so he contacted Cynthia to write some press materials, direct sales and marketing copy, phone scripts, and website blogs.

At first, all seemed fine. Derrick said he liked the material Cynthia prepared after she worked for two days on it. He paid her by a credit card, and asked her to do more, in time for a trade show he planned to enter. So she canceled her own plans for the day to meet his deadline, worked for about four hours writing additional marketing material. She sent it by email as before, and as before she charged his credit card. However, this time it was declined.

After she told him this, he assured her that paying her would be a priority, but then came several excuses. First, his wife had trouble finding another credit card that wasn't maxed out. Then, she claimed she tore up a new card by mistake, and it would take 10 days to get another card. After that, Derrick indicated he was having some financial difficulties, and he asked if Cynthia would she take the balance due in trade. After Cynthia told him no, since there was nothing she wanted to trade for, she offered to accept payments of $100 a month. But her offer got no response, and Derrick didn't reply to a few voice mails she left for him.

Then, about 6 weeks later, she suddenly got a chargeback complaint from her merchant account on which she had charged his first payment, in which Derrick was claiming fraud, on the grounds he had not authorized or participated in the transaction. She sent him an email, saying there must be some mistake, but received no response again. After she responded to her merchant account service with copies of all the correspondence back and forth showing Derrick's original copy, her changes, and his approvals, along with his email about making paying her a priority, her bank reversed the chargeback. Again, Derrick again lied to his own bank to claim no authorization and that he was not a party to the transaction. So his bank reversed the chargeback reversal, because the way the laws are written, the customer is given the benefit of the doubt in claiming fraud, even though the customer is actually the one committing fraud. Unfortunately, Cynthia didn't have a formally signed contract or signed receipt of materials delivered, since all their communication had been by email and phone. So despite all her evidence of carrying out the work for Derrick successfully, she lost, and Derrick gained all her work for nothing. And later she saw he actually used it in the press releases and marketing pitches he sent out.

Only in retrospect did Cynthia realize there had been some warning signs leading up to Derrick's actions. He was having financial difficulties due to the slowdown in his business. He had parted ways with a former partner, who he claimed had simply left and taken his name off the business, because his partner wanted to do something else. But when Cynthia later spoke to the partner, he said he had left because he was uncomfortable with some of the unethical things Derrick was doing, such as when Derrick unilaterally sent out sales pitches with false information about how he could save or make people money. Thus, the partner just wanted out. And then, Cynthia realized that some of the material she had written for Derrick contained false and misleading information, though she didn't notice this at the time, since she wasn't a knowledgeable expert in financial matters.

So what might Cynthia have done in the first place to avoid this problem – and what should you do in dealing with a client who is dishonest?

1 You should work on a retainer or payment in advance basis, except in working with large, established companies that usually have a 30 day or 60 day payment after invoice policy.

2. You should notice if prospective clients are having financial difficulties, such as if they are experiencing a slow-down in their business. If so, you should go over the financial costs of your services and make sure clients understand that these payments will be required before you provide the service.

3. Ask clients to sign a contract in which they acknowledge the costs, give you the go ahead to provide certain services at a predetermined cost or hourly rate, and understand that there are no refunds for the work that is completed.

4. Send any work to clients, so the client has to sign for it by mail or has to acknowledge receipt if the work is emailed or faxed.

5. Be cautious in working or continuing to work with a client if that client is asking you to write up material with false information or claims, since this suggests you are working with an individual who is fundamentally dishonest.

6. Consider filing a small claims suit if the amount is large enough, though you may not want to face down a deadbeat who lies in court – or invest the time in fighting the case.

7. Report what the individual did to the appropriate agencies, such as to a professional certification board or association, if the person has to be certified for their work, such as filing a complaint with the bar association if the person is a lawyer. You can also file a report for the record with the police department where you live or have your offices, as well as where the criminal client lives or works.

CHAPTER 14: WHEN YOU DISCOVER A CLIENT HAS DONE SOMETHING UNETHICAL OR IMMORAL

What should you do if you discover that a client has done something unethical or immoral, based on their code of professional conduct or your religious and moral beliefs? While the action may not be criminal, you find it inappropriate behavior that could open the client up to civil litigation or censure by their professional organization, should their behavior become known. Once you know, what duty do you have to tell anyone? In some cases the law is clear cut, such as if you discover that a client is abusing a child or is threatening to harm a particular person. In other cases, you have no duty to act, but should you act to expose that person? And should you continue to work with that client?

That was the issue which faced Brenda, who was working as a life coach. Mostly she helped clients assess their personal and work life, decide on their goals, consider how satisfied they were with their current circumstances, and otherwise get what they wanted out of life. Generally, she found the work very fulfilling, especially when she helped clients determine their path in life and gain fulfillment from their daily activities and relationships. She also liked guiding and supporting clients as they made difficult choices to drop toxic relationships and acquire new ones that made them feel better about themselves.

By contrast, she found it difficult to work with Caroline in their weekly sessions. Though Caroline helped her own clients deal with day-to-day family problems as a marriage and family therapist, Brenda found that Caroline was conflicted about what she really wanted to do, as well as involved in a tumultuous relationship with an on-again off-again boyfriend. "But dealing with those issues makes me a better therapist," Caroline told her. "Since I have my own problems in these areas, I can better relate to my clients and help them solve their problems, even though I have difficulty resolving my own issues because I'm so emotionally invested in them."

These explanations seemed to reflect a reasonable way of dealing with these problems, so Brenda accepted Caroline's choices. At the same time, Brenda worked with Caroline on finding a clear career path, since Caroline wanted to expand what she was already doing in other directions. She was especially interested in speaking, doing workshops and seminars, writing books, and becoming a radio host and TV interviewer. So their weekly sessions were devoted to exploring these different options and what Caroline should do to realize her dreams.

Brenda had noticed a few warning signs when she first began working with Caroline, such as when Caroline told her "I'm a control freak." But at the time, a single warning wasn't enough to pull back from working together. Instead, she adapted to this declaration by letting Caroline set the agenda for what they would discuss and making sure that Caroline felt comfortable with the issues they talked about. Brenda also was flexible when Caroline wanted to shift their meeting times to accommodate her schedule with her clients.

But one day, while she was sitting in Caroline's office, about to begin a session, Caroline got a call from her attorney, and Brenda could hear their discussion. From what she heard, she soon realized that Caroline was in deep trouble with her professional licensing association, which was considering withdrawing their certification, so she could lose her license. Moreover, Brenda discovered that Caroline was facing two lawsuits from unhappy clients. In one case, Caroline had borrowed $35,000 from her client's parents, promising to pay it back. She claimed that she needed the money to pay her office rent, which was going up, and that she needed to pay this to keep her office in the city in order to continue treating their daughter, who was experiencing a major crisis over her abusive husband and child. But after a year of borrowing this money, Brenda still hadn't paid back Caroline's parents. She hadn't even made any payments, though she bought some very expensive dresses and jewelry to keep up appearances. In another case, Caroline had persuaded a patient who was extremely overweight to work in her office for free on the grounds that this would help her self-esteem, since she couldn't find a job because of her weight. But then the patient only felt worse and quit both the job and the therapy, and it was a conflict of interest for Caroline to get a patient in therapy to work for free. Later, realizing that Caroline had exploited them, both patients had complained to the licensing agency, and, as Brenda listened, Caroline discussed how the lawyer could help her save her license as well as settle the suits.

Meanwhile, as she listened to Caroline reveal these private concerns, Brenda felt repulsed by what her client had done. She felt that if she was judging the case, Caroline should not only lose her license but lose any lawsuit against her, and she debated whether to continue to work with Caroline or not, or whether, as a life coach, she should counsel Brenda on avoiding such compromising situations in the future.

After Caroline got off the phone, apologizing for taking time away from their session, Brenda acted like nothing had happened and continued the discussion of Brenda's life choices and where to go next. But after she left, she felt very bothered by what she had heard and what to do about it. Fortunately Caroline solved Brenda's problem by postponing the next few sessions and finally telling her that she didn't have the money to continue to meet, though Brenda wondered if she had handled the situation the right way when she first learned about it.

What should Brenda have done to avoid this problem – and what should you do in dealing with a client when you discover that the client has done something that violates your ethical or moral principles?

1) Brenda should realize that there are some things about a client it may not be possible to know in advance; they may only come out during the working relationship. So Brenda should not blame herself for not realizing her client was involved in unethical behavior or behavior she considered immoral.

2) If the client raises red flags early on when describing his or her background, concerns, and expectations, ask more questions to determine if this is a good fit, such as when Caroline described herself as a "control freak." Brenda might have asked Caroline to explain more, such as by giving examples of how she acted in this way with her own clients, and discuss how this might affect their working together. Then, if it seems these qualities could present a problem in working together, as opposed to simply selling that client's merchandise, gracefully back away from doing further work together.

3) If you discover the client is involved in something you consider unethical or immoral while working for the client, consider what you have learned confidential, unless you are legally required to report such behavior, such as if it involves child abuse or a threat to injure a specific person.

4) If you discover this negative information about a client from a public source, such as a post on the social media, first check out the veracity of this information. If accurate, you can feel free to talk about your knowledge of this public information to others, such as if you are asked to give a reference about this client to another person. Or if you prefer, don't say anything, and don't give a reference.

5) If you aren't sure whether to continue to work with the client or not based on what you have heard or learned from others, you might have a discussion with that person, if appropriate, about these issues and explain why you feel you can't work with him or her anymore. But if you feel uncomfortable about giving an explanation, it is probably best to simply gracefully withdraw from further work with that person, and give a neutral reason, such as having an overcommitted schedule.

6) Decide if you can continue working with a person who is involved in behavior you consider unethical or moral, though not criminal, depending on the nature of your work together and how problematic you consider this person's behavior. For example, if you are providing products, rather than services, or a less personalized service, such as providing insurance or a mortgage for

someone, a person's ethical or moral actions may be less relevant, and you don't want to discriminate in providing your services. However, if your services are more personal, such as being a therapist or life coach, your relationship with the person does matter, and it may be best to withdraw if you experience a serious conflict with your own values.

7) If appropriate and you feel comfortable doing so, tell the client what you consider unethical behavior, since this might give the client a chance to explain or change.

8) If you feel you can no longer work with the client, whether or not you have told the client why and given the client a chance to explain, advise the client that you can no longer work together. If you can, diplomatically tell the client why, such as saying: "If don't feel I can help you, since we have very different points of view," or "I don't feel we are a good fit for working together, since our attitudes are so different." Or just offer a general excuse, such as having a scheduling problem in seeing that client again.

9) Once you stop working with a client, avoid naming the client you had a problem with if you describe the situation to avoid problems of defamation or libel, and to avoid giving prospective clients or referrals a sense that you talk about previous clients. However, you can talk about the problem in general or disguise the client's name and identifying details in describing what happened.

PART VII: OTHER ISSUES

CHAPTER 15: WHEN A CLIENT HAS DIFFERENT BELIEFS FROM YOU

Sometimes professionals and merchants with deeply held beliefs run into people with very different beliefs who want to use their services or products. However, they believe due to their strong faith that they shouldn't do anything to support a lifestyle which goes against their religious tenets. They may even discover the information after they start working with a client, and suddenly feel that they shouldn't continue to work together, and that the right thing to do is to return the client's money and explain why they can't work with that person. Or should they do that?

Such a personal crisis of faith happened to Rebecca, the owner of a bridal shop, who had recently had an after-hours mixer at her shop that was organized through a local merchant's association. Several dozen people showed up to mingle over snacks and wine, and even some local officials made an appearance to honor her business for hosting the event, so she felt very proud to be considered a leader in the community.

That event is also where she met Nanette who told her she planned to get married in a few months, though her future husband, a lawyer, wasn't able to attend due to dealing with an important case. Could Rebecca design and fit a wedding dress for her? Immediately, Rebecca told Nanette that she would be pleased and honored to do so. Thus, after getting a deposit for half of the finished dress, the rest due on completion, she reviewed several designs, cut the fabric, and began fitting the dress on Nanette.

However, while admiring the dress in the mirror, Nanette mentioned that her future husband planned to come in that weekend to see the beginnings of the dress, before Rebecca added additional lace and other finishing touches. Then, Nanette mentioned her husband's name, Jane, and noted that many members of the local LGBQT community would be attending from out of state. So Nanette gushed about how thrilled she was that such weddings were now legal in the state.

Though Rebecca didn't want to show it, she was appalled by the idea of creating a wedding dress for a lesbian wedding, since she was a strong believer as a Christian and church goer at an evangelical church which considered homosexuality a sin. Even though she had already put over 20 hours into creating the dress, she was ready to return Nanette's deposit and explain why she couldn't make her dress. But that night, when she spoke to her sister, who was a member of her church, on the phone, her sister told her she had to complete the dress. "You can't discriminate against your customers. That's not right." Though her sister agreed that Rebecca could and should make such choices in her personal life, such as choosing her friends and who she might marry, she couldn't do so in her work. In fact, her sister warned her, if Rebecca did, others in the business community might learn of her actions and they might look unfavorably on her. So this could harm her reputation, too. Plus she might lose business from others in the large LGTBQ community in the area, which could undermine her service. So Rebecca did complete the dress and said nothing to Nanette about her reservations, though she continued to wrestle in her consciences about whether she had done the right thing.

Did Rebecca do the right thing – and what should you do if you are faced with working with a client who has a lifestyle that conflicts with your strongly held religious beliefs of what is right and wrong?

1) While as a business owner you have the right to choose your own clients and feel good about who you choose to do business with, so you should not be forced to serve anyone. At the same time, you need to recognize that your business is one that should serve the whole community. Thus, unless a client has done or is doing something criminal and unethical, you should normally provide your service or products to that client.

2) You need to separate your own lifestyle choices based on your beliefs from the lifestyle choices of your clients. You are not undermining your own beliefs when you serve or sell products to someone who has a different lifestyle, since your service or sale

does not represent an endorsement of this other lifestyle. You are simply providing the service or product to this client, just like you would any other client.

3) As an alternative, if you know in advance that a prospective client has a lifestyle or beliefs that go against your own values, you might refer that person on to a competitor by suggesting that they might do a better job, that you are too busy with other clients now, or some other diplomatic reason. But don't insult that person's choices. However, if you have already accepted the project, continue to work on it, and put your own beliefs aside. Remind yourself this is strictly a business agreement and do your best work as you would for any other client.

4) If you don't provide a service or product to a client based on your beliefs, this choice might be frowned upon by others in the community who value toleration, whether they are members of the particular group you are discriminating against, which could damage your business.

5) If you discriminate based on someone's lifestyle which is neither criminal or unethical, you risk a lawsuit against you for discrimination, and in most cases, those filing these discrimination suits have won. Moreover, win or lose, this will be very costly for you to fight against, and you are likely to have national representatives fighting discrimination helping the client you have discriminated against. Plus you may be featured in the media as a result of your actions, and generally most of the media will be sympathetic to your client and present you and your business in a negative light.

6) If you need to feel better about acting in a way that you think is against your faith, talk to others in your faith who agree that it is not right to discriminate, much like Rebecca talked to her sister.

7) Take some other action to feel better about your choice, such as talking to an understanding religious leader or praying to reassure yourself that you have done the right thing by not discriminating against someone who has a different faith or lifestyle.

8) Remind yourself that you live in a community that values diversity, so you are not really dealing with an impossible client. Rather, you have created an impossible situation for yourself by not recognizing that you can separate your personal beliefs and choices from your responsibilities as a professional or retailer who is in business to serve a diverse clientele.

ABOUT THE AUTHOR

GINI GRAHAM SCOTT, Ph.D., J.D., is a nationally known writer, consultant, speaker, and seminar leader, specializing in business and work relationships, professional and personal development, social trends, and popular culture. She has published over 50 books on diverse subjects with major publishers. She has worked with dozens of clients on memoirs, self-help, and popular business books, as well as film scripts. Writing samples are at www.ginigrahamscott.com and www.changemakerspublishingandwriting.com. She is a Huffington Post regular columnist, commenting on social trends, new technology, business, and everyday life at www.huffingtonpost.com/gini-graham-scott.

She is the founder of Changemakers Publishing featuring books on work, business, psychology, social trends, and self-help, which has published over 40 Print, Ebooks, and Audiobooks. She has licensed several dozen books for foreign sales, including the UK, Russia, Korea, Spain, Indonesia, and Japan.

She has received national media exposure for her books, including appearances on *Good Morning America, Oprah, Montel Williams,* and *CNN*. She has been the producer and host of a talk show series, CHANGEMAKERS, featuring interviews on social trends.

Her books on business relationships and professional development include:

Turn Your Dreams into Reality (Llewellyn)
Resolving Conflict (Changemakers Publishing)
A Survival Guide for Working with Bad Bosses (AMACOM)

A Survival Guide for Working with Humans (AMACOM)

Making Ethical Choices, Resolving Ethical Dilemmas (Changemakers Publishing)

Credit Card Fraud with Jen Grondahl Lee (Rowman)

Her books on social trends and popular culture include:

American Justice with Paul Brakke (Touchpoint Press)

Scammed (Allworth Press)

The New Middle Ages (Nortia Press)

Internet Book Piracy (Allworth Press)

Lies and Liars: How and Why Sociopaths Lie (Skyhorse Publishing)

Scott is also active in a number of community and business groups, including the Lafayette and Danville Chambers of Commerce. She is a graduate of the prestigious Leadership in Contra Costa County program, is a member of B2B groups in Danville and Walnut Creek, a BNI member, and a member of Lafayette Savvy Women. She is the organizer of six Meetup groups in the film and publishing industries with over 5000 members in Los Angeles and the San Francisco Bay Area. She does workshops and seminars on the topics of her books.

She received her Ph.D. from the University of California, Berkeley, and her J.D. from the University of San Francisco Law School. She has received several MAs at Cal State, East Bay, and is getting an additional MA in Communications in 2017.

CHANGEMAKERS PUBLISHING

3527 Mt. Diablo Blvd., #273
Lafayette, CA 94549
changemakers@pacbell.net . (925) 385-0608
www.changemakerspublishingandwriting.com

www.ingramcontent.com/pod-product-compliance
Lightning Source LLC
Chambersburg PA
CBHW071501210326
41597CB00018B/2651